The Usborne Book of the
MOON

Written by LAURA COWAN

Illustrated by DIANA TOLEDANO
Designed by ZOE WRAY

Expert advice from Brendan Owens and Emily Drabek-Maunder
from the Royal Observatory Greenwich, and Stuart Atkinson

It's a clear night.
The Sun has set and the Moon has risen.

Tonight, it's beautiful, **big and round**,
lighting up the sky and shimmering in the sea.

But, here the Moon looks like a sideways smile in the sky.

Why has it changed shape and how?

There are LOTS of things to wonder about our mysterious Moon...

Where is it?
Can I visit it?

What makes it shine?

How old is it?
How big is it?
Can I touch it?

Does the Moon have a face?

Does anyone live there?

Hellooo, anyone home?

Does anything grow there?

Is it alive?

Can I shoot an arrow or throw a ball and make the Moon fall out of the sky?

I've heard it's made of cheese. Is it?

Yum, yum.

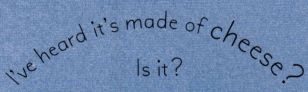

Sometimes the Moon looks near enough to touch, but it's actually very, VERY far away.

EARTH
(the planet where we live)

If you could drive a car to the Moon, it would take almost five months, driving at TOP SPEED all the way!

Brummmmmmmmm

Even in a rocket, it takes three whole days to reach the Moon from Earth.

SPACE
(everything from 100km (62 miles) above the Earth)

THE SUN

is A LOT further away than the Moon. It would take nearly 200 years to drive there in a car.

THE MOON

goes around, or ORBITS, the Earth.

The Sun gives the Earth and the Moon light. Sunlight reflects off the Moon. That's what makes it seem to SHINE at night.

The Moon's orbit takes just under a month, or 27.3 days to be exact.

The Earth and Moon ORBIT the Sun together. Their orbit takes a whole year. Well, actually it's 365.25 days.

On Earth, every night, the Moon looks a little different.
Some nights it looks HUGE...

...and some nights it looks
as though the Moon
ISN'T THERE AT ALL.

There are different
names for each size
or SHAPE of the Moon.

Sometimes you can see
the Moon in daytime.

QUARTER

CRESCENT

NEW MOON

I can't see the Moon.
IS IT DEAD?!
HAS SOMEONE STOLEN IT?!

It's still there, but the side lit up
by the Sun is facing away from us.

As the Moon travels around
the Earth, we see more or
less of its lit side.

So, that's why it seems
to change shape.

GIBBOUS

Gibbon?

NO! Gibbous!

It seems to grow bigger
and bigger
and bigger
until it's a...

FULL MOON

The night after the full moon,
the Moon looks a little smaller, with
just a tiny sliver missing. And then the
next night it's a little smaller still.
Until you can't see it at all – then it
starts to grow all over again.

For many years, THOUSANDS of years,
people looked at the Moon, and wondered WHAT it was and
WHERE it came from. But... there was no way to find out.
So, they made up their own stories.

According to people
in FINLAND...

...once, a giant bird
laid six eggs on
the goddess
Ilmatar's knees.
They fell and
CRACKED!

The whites became the
Moon and stars.

The yolks
became
the Sun.

The shells
became the
Earth and sky.

People in EAST AFRICA said...

...the Moon was pale and dull until it stole a fire feather from the Sun.

The Sun was angry and splattered the Moon with mud, which is why the Moon has spots.

The Slavic people of EASTERN EUROPE had different stories.

Some said the Moon was the Sun's bald uncle...

...others said the Moon was a beautiful goddess.

For some people in CENTRAL AFRICA, the story went...

...once there were two suns in the sky.

But, they made too much light and heat for everyone on Earth.

So, one of the suns tricked the other into going for a swim.

The water put out most of its light. And so it became... the Moon.

Let's bathe in this lovely river!

Whee!

In other places, when people looked at the Moon, they saw... a rabbit.

Once, according to the people of CENTRAL AMERICA,
the snake god Quetzalcoatl became human and
wandered the Earth...

I'm so weak
with hunger.
Do you have
any food?

Why don't you eat
some of this grass
with me?

I can't eat grass.
It will make me sick!

Then you can eat me instead.
I have nothing else to offer.

Of course, Quetzalcoatl did not
eat the little rabbit. Instead he raised
him to the Moon and left his image
there, so everyone would see it and
remember the rabbit's kindness.

In EAST ASIA, people came up with similar stories about the rabbit they could see on the Moon. In the Chinese version, a goddess lives there too.

Once, a goddess named Chang'e married a man on Earth and became human.

But she changed her mind.

So, she drank a magic potion that turned her back into a goddess...

...and she floated all the way to the Moon...

Wheeeeeee

...where she has lived with the rabbit ever since.

In 2019, a Chinese spacecraft landed on the far side of the Moon. The spacecraft was called Chang'e 4.

Some people realized the Moon was not just good for stories but useful, too. Around the world, people saw that a FULL MOON came around every 29.5 days and they could use this cycle to track time.

Early people made marks on animal bones to keep records of moon cycles.

Is it nearly summer yet?

Not according to the bone!

FULL MOON tomorrow! All the better for spotting boar on our night hunt.

In Egypt, thousands of years ago, people known as ASTRONOMERS studied the skies.

They also saw that there was a FULL MOON every 29 days or so and they made a CALENDAR from the cycle.

Egyptians used this moon calendar to mark their festivals.

Time to celebrate the Jubilee of Nut! Wheeeeeeee!

Early Jewish people used a similar moon calendar. According to the Jewish bible, the NEW MOON was a special occasion.

Blow the horns for the new month!

I spy the new moon!

In China, astronomers used the Moon to track time, too.
They also wanted to know if there was going to be...

AN ECLIPSE

An eclipse happens when the Moon
moves between the Sun and Earth.
The Moon blocks out some
of the Sun...

...or ALL of it in a total eclipse.
On a bright day, the sky could
go as DARK as NIGHT.

Sun ---->

Moon ----->

Total eclipses happen about once every 18 months, but they can only
be seen from the same place roughly once every 375 years.

What are
you doing?

I'm calculating
eclipses for the next
hundred years.

But WHY?

Because it is an
important message from
the sky for the Emperor!

Thinkers and astronomers everywhere wanted to understand more about the Moon. Over many years, they came up with ideas they believed were true, but couldn't prove... yet.
They even made instruments to help them.

In ANCIENT GREECE and the ROMAN EMPIRE...

Chairete!
(That's Ancient Greek for hello!)
I'm Anaxagoras. Hmmm, where does the Moon get its light from?
I think it's the SUN that makes the Moon shine.

Um, no?
It's the gods, of course!

I'm Plutarch and I've been reading A LOT about the Moon.
Some people think the Sun goes around the Earth,

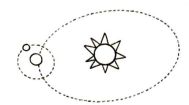

I say WE go around the Sun, and, I say the Moon goes around US.

Maybe only one side of the Moon is ever lit by the Sun.

Also, are those spots VALLEYS? I wonder if anyone lives there? Are there cities?

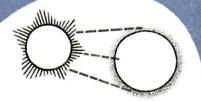

In the MIDDLE EAST...

My name is Mariam al-Asturlabi and I lived in Syria over a thousand years ago. I am famous for making instruments called astrolabes.

Astrolabes are used to measure the positions of the Moon and stars in the sky.

In INDIA...

I'm reading the **Surya Siddhanta.** It tells me how big the Moon is...

...how long its orbit is...

...and even how far away from Earth it is.

When people finally had the technology to check all these ideas, it turned out...
A LOT OF THEM WERE RIGHT.

For hundreds of years, astronomers watched the skies. Everything seemed small and a LONG way away, until... in 1608, a German-Dutch spectacle maker named Hans Lippershey made a **super** new instrument for seeing faraway things UP CLOSE. It was called... a telescope.

About a year later...

Thomas Harriot
England, July, 1609

I saw a comet in the sky last year. It was MAGNIFICENT! Now I've bought a telescope so I can look at the Moon in more detail.

I've drawn a picture of what the Moon's surface looks like through my telescope.

Galileo Galilei
Italy, November, 1609

I heard about these new telescopes in Venice! So I built my own version. I think it's a LOT better.

I'm going to write a book to tell everyone what I can see! It's FANTASTIC!

Galileo sent his Moon book out into the world and it changed the way people thought about space forever.

The Moon isn't a perfect silver sphere at all!

There are mountains and valleys and craters, but where are all the cities and people?

So, at last, people could see the Moon was a REAL place. And a few started to think one day we could go there...

Scientists made bigger and **bigger** telescopes that could see further and **further**. Some were built in places called observatories, specially designed for studying the skies – but others were just in wealthy people's gardens.

WOAH!

I feel as if I'm ON the Moon when I look at it through your HUGE telescope.

As well as finding new ways of looking at the Moon, scientists were experimenting with new ways of creating **pictures** of it, too.

French artist Louis Daguerre helped create a process for taking photos. In 1839, he tried to take a picture of the Moon.

Can I take a photo of the MOON with this camera? Through this telescope?

This is really hard. It's all blurred.

A year later, in New York, a scientist named John William Draper used Daguerre's invention...

That's it!

Each photo took 20 minutes to take.

The world was changing fast. Impossible things were becoming possible. Until the 1800s, horseback was the fastest way to travel. But soon inventions came along that could go A LOT faster.

There were steam ships to cross the oceans.

There were trains and cars that could whoosh over land.

Soon there would be flying machines in the skies.

Do you think some day we'll be able to travel to... THE MOON?

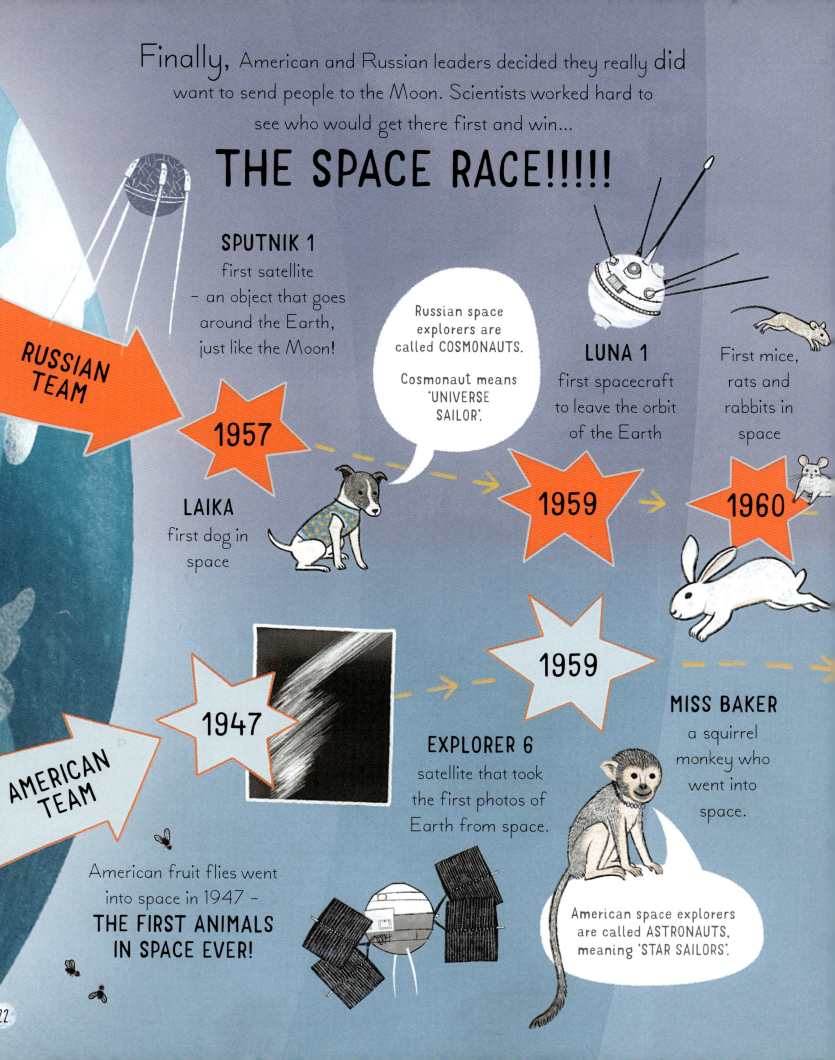

Finally, American and Russian leaders decided they really **did** want to send people to the Moon. Scientists worked hard to see who would get there first and win...

THE SPACE RACE!!!!!

RUSSIAN TEAM

SPUTNIK 1
first satellite – an object that goes around the Earth, just like the Moon!

Russian space explorers are called COSMONAUTS.

Cosmonaut means 'UNIVERSE SAILOR'.

LUNA 1
first spacecraft to leave the orbit of the Earth

First mice, rats and rabbits in space

1957

LAIKA
first dog in space

1959

1960

1959

MISS BAKER
a squirrel monkey who went into space.

AMERICAN TEAM

1947

EXPLORER 6
satellite that took the first photos of Earth from space.

American fruit flies went into space in 1947 –
THE FIRST ANIMALS IN SPACE EVER!

American space explorers are called ASTRONAUTS, meaning 'STAR SAILORS'.

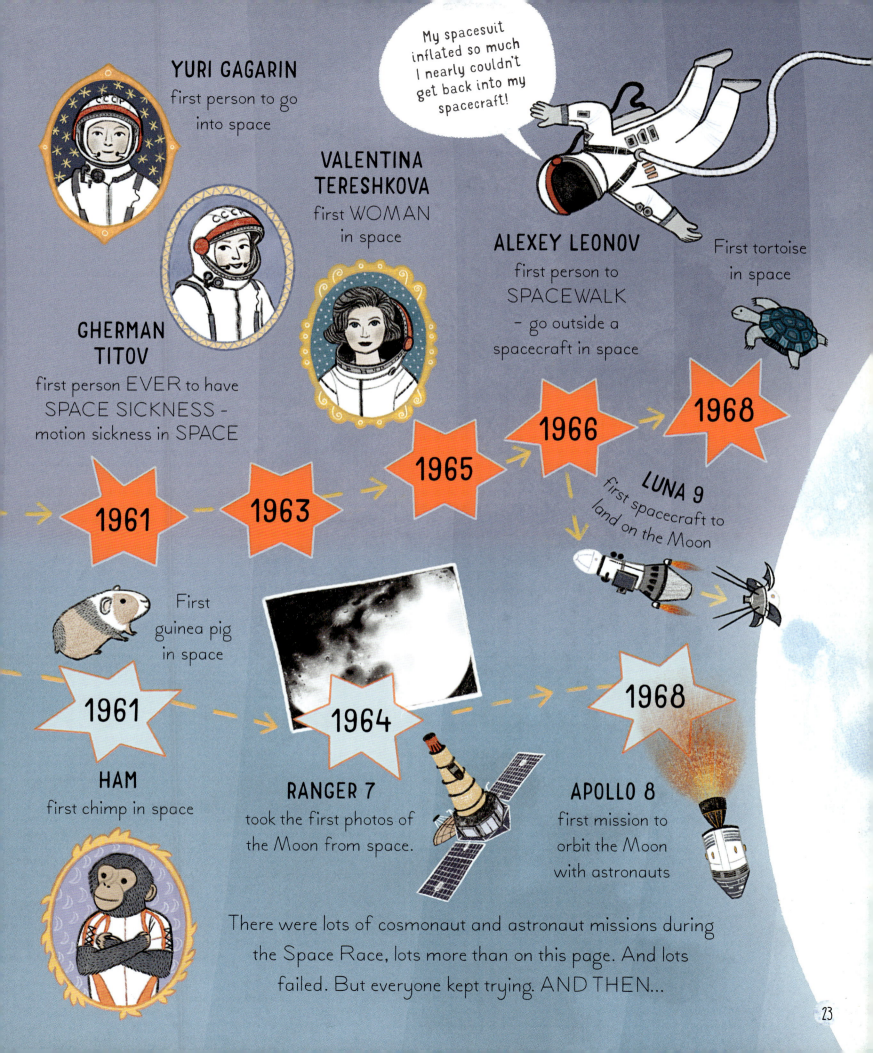

YURI GAGARIN
first person to go into space

VALENTINA TERESHKOVA
first WOMAN in space

My spacesuit inflated so much I nearly couldn't get back into my spacecraft!

ALEXEY LEONOV
first person to SPACEWALK – go outside a spacecraft in space

First tortoise in space

GHERMAN TITOV
first person EVER to have SPACE SICKNESS – motion sickness in SPACE

1961 – **1963** → **1965** → **1966** → **1968**

LUNA 9
first spacecraft to land on the Moon

First guinea pig in space

1961 → **1964** → **1968**

HAM
first chimp in space

RANGER 7
took the first photos of the Moon from space.

APOLLO 8
first mission to orbit the Moon with astronauts

There were lots of cosmonaut and astronaut missions during the Space Race, lots more than on this page. And lots failed. But everyone kept trying. AND THEN...

On July 16th, 1969, at 09:32, the Americans launched Apollo 11. Inside were three astronauts, Edwin "Buzz" Aldrin, Neil Armstrong and Michael "Mike" Collins, hoping to get to the Moon...

400,000 people helped get the mission ready – there was a lot to do!

Scientists CALCULATED the journey to the Moon, and how to land on the surface – as well as get off it again!

Technicians MADE equipment...

...and PREPARED scientific experiments.

Engineers BUILT spacecraft.

And a MILLION people gathered to watch the launch at Cape Kennedy, Florida.

COLUMBIA, the Command and Service Modules to carry the astronauts into space, and EAGLE, the Lunar Module to land on the Moon, are housed here.

SATURN V, the rocket with the fuel to shoot them into space!

LIFT OFF!
We have a lift-off, at 32 minutes past the hour. Lift off on Apollo 11!

It was a long journey. But the three astronauts were always in touch with MISSION CONTROL, in Houston, Texas, to help them make calculations and just to chat...

Eagle

Columbia

CONTROL Houston

COLUMBIA

Watch for a lovely girl with a big rabbit.

An ancient legend says a beautiful Chinese girl called Chang'e has been living there for 4,000 years.

Okay. We'll keep a close eye out for the bunny girl.

When they reached the Moon, COLUMBIA and EAGLE stayed in orbit for a day and the astronauts looked for a good place to land.

On July 20th, Mike stayed aboard COLUMBIA, while Buzz and Neil took EAGLE down to the Moon's surface. And at 20:17...

Back on Earth, nearly 600 million people all over the world were watching on their televisions.

Houston, TRANQUILITY BASE here. The EAGLE has landed.

100 hours and 42 minutes

after launch – and four hours after landing –
Neil Armstrong climbed out...

That's one small step for a man, one giant leap for mankind...

Buzz and Neil spent just TWO HOURS outside on the Moon's surface. Still, they managed to get a lot done, before heading home...

They took photos and set up a camera to film everything, so everyone on Earth could watch, too.

"Be advised there're lots of smiling faces in this room and all over the world. Over."

Mission Control talked to them while they set up experiments and collected samples of MOON DUST and ROCK. The astronauts found...

...rocks that show some of the Moon is OLDER than Earth!

...holes and craters AS BIG AS CITIES made from flying space rocks, called meteors.

...NO wind or rain or even AIR so Buzz and Neil's footprints are still on the Moon.

AND NO CHEESE!

Back on EAGLE, they were ready to go when, UH-OH... what's that on the floor?

If that switch is broken, we can't blast off!

Mission Control told Buzz and Neil to get some sleep while they solved the problem... except they couldn't.

The next morning, Buzz had an idea...

Maybe, my PEN can be the switch...

Thanks to Buzz's pen, they managed to take off and join Mike on the COLUMBIA.

EAGLE'S landing gear was left behind on the Moon.

POP!

Then they flew back to Earth and SPLASHED DOWN in the Pacific Ocean...

Whrrrrrrrreeee

...where the American President, Richard Nixon, was waiting on the USS Hornet to congratulate them.

After Apollo 11, five more Apollo missions landed on the Moon, but nobody has walked on its surface since 1972. Will people go to the Moon again? What will happen next?

Some scientists want to build a LUNAR GATEWAY to orbit the Moon - a spaceport, like an airport but in space!

Beep! Beep! I'm a lunar robot...

Well, you should know there is no sound in space, so there's no point beeping at me.

Next stop... Pluto!

One day, maybe, we could stop off there on the way to MARS or even FURTHER.

Other scientists want to build a place to live ON the Moon - a LUNAR COLONY.

People could LEARN about living in space, but still know they were only three days from home.

There would be a lot to get used to - a night on the Moon lasts 354 hours!

The Moon is slowly, SLOWLY drifting away from Earth, so that in billions of years' time its orbit will be much bigger. But, before that happens, we might have left Earth and our Moon behind to explore new worlds.

GOODBYE, MOON! THANK YOU FOR EVERYTHING!

INDEX

USBORNE QUICKLINKS

For links to websites where you can find out more about the Moon, see amazing images and watch video clips, visit the Usborne Quicklinks website. Here are some of the things you can do at the sites we recommend:

- See what the Moon looks like through a telescope
- Learn lots of amazing facts about the Moon
- Watch a video clip about the first Moon landing
- See Neil Armstrong walk on the Moon

To visit these sites, go to www.usborne.com/quicklinks and type in the title of this book. Children should be supervised online. Please read the online safety guidelines at the Usborne Quicklinks website.

Edited by Ruth Brocklehurst
Digital manipulation: John Russell

Thanks to Nickey Butler

First published in 2019 by Usborne Publishing Ltd., Usborne House, 83-85 Saffron Hill, London EC1N 8RT, England. Copyright © 2019 Usborne Publishing Ltd. The name Usborne and the devices ⊕⊕ are Trade Marks of Usborne Publishing Ltd. All rights reserved. No part of this publication may be reproduced, stored in a retrieval system or transmitted in any form or by any means, electronic, mechanical, photocopying, recording, or otherwise, without previous permission of the publisher. Printed in UAE. UE.